MW01617755

Regarding the Cross

ISBN 0-9768611-0-0

Author, photographer, artist, and layout designer
William R. Wolfram

The Center for Liturgical Art
Concordia University
800 North Columbia Avenue
Seward, Nebraska 68434

Biblical quotations are from the New American Standard Bible.
A J Holman Company, Philadelphia and New York

PRINTED IN THE UNITED STATES OF AMERICA
Marathon Press of Norfolk, Nebraska

August 2005

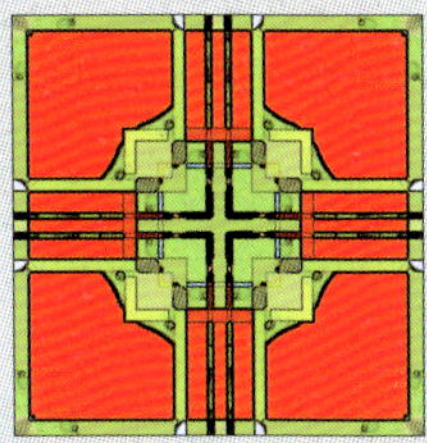

Regarding the Cross

William R. Wolfram

Many of the photographs used for the composition
of this book's crosses were taken at Hughes Brothers, Incorporated
and the farm of Bill and Doris Hartmann,
both in Seward County, Nebraska.

The mission of The Center for Liturgical Art is to promote the use of exceptional visual art in worship and ministry.

The staff and faculty of The Center for Liturgical Art
and the Concordia University, Nebraska Department of Art
are available to churches and congregations
for presentations, consultations, and training seminars.
The Center also accepts commissions for liturgical art as it works
with individuals to enhance the silent witness
of the visual arts in worship and ministry.

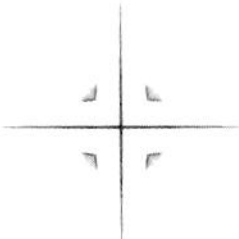

Foreword

William Wolfram invites us to consider the Cross of Christ in common, everyday objects, though his images, text, and scripture passages go beyond this invitation. They beckon and challenge us to look more closely at the love and mystery of God through the work of His Son, Jesus Christ.

In the opening remarks we read, ". . . faith sees beauty in this ugly piece of wood." And so it is. William Wolfram arranges ordinary, mundane objects and surfaces and, with the intelligent eye of the artist, sees beauty. He transforms the ordinary to the extraordinary and beckons us to perceive in a new way – to look beyond the surface, to delight in the subtle ironies and inner beauty of those common objects in our everyday experience. This book is a metaphor for the beauty of salvation itself. A baby, born of a virgin in a lowly stable and first worshipped by shepherds, is the object and fulfillment of God's beautiful plan of salvation.

We are reminded that the outcast, the worn, and those in need are the very ones whom Christ makes beautiful and acceptable before God through His death on the Cross. The truth of faith appears when we see the beauty of salvation in that "ugly piece of wood." May this work of love delight the eyes and stir the heart to acknowledge the mystery and majesty of God as He continues to work His miracles in our lives.

Kenneth E. Schmidt, Director
The Center for Liturgical Art
2005

Regarding the Cross

Understanding the Cross of Christ is the only way we can fathom the person of Jesus Christ. It is vital in comprehending why He visited earth to become our Savior. Jesus is more than a moral teacher. He is the Redeemer. The message of the Cross, therefore, has become the central doctrine of Christians everywhere.

Believers show affection and admiration for the Cross, whereas skeptics usually exhibit contempt for it. Faith sees beauty in this ugly piece of wood, a view that separates Christians from unbelievers. Truly, God has revealed His heart at Calvary's Cross.

The early church chose the Cross as its central symbol even though the Cross was associated with criminal executions and derided by scoffers. Jesus, more than anything, wanted to be remembered by His death. He forewarned His disciples about His imminent death and memorialized it in the upper room. Indeed, the Cross was foremost on His mind. In faithfulness to their Savior, the early Christians endured the scorn of the heathen.

The crosses presented in this work invite the reader to meditate upon the Cross, to survey it, and to see it from many viewpoints. Each cross encourages the viewer to discover and imagine. The pictures are abstract, digital manipulations coupled with annotations that prompt us to explore the great panorama of God's love through the events of the crucifixion.

Pictorial representation, or realism, imposes the artist's point of view, whereas, abstraction removes the tangible and absolute. The crosses presented here give nondirective messages. The crosses show diverse colors, textures, and shapes. Uniquely designed, each cross evokes different thoughts about God's love as revealed in His great redemptive act. Allow the crosses and occasional commentary to be a starting point for personal meditations on the Cross of Christ.

4

But now apart from the Law the righteousness of God has been manifested, being witnessed by the Law and the Prophets, even the righteousness of God through faith in Jesus Christ for all those who believe; for there is no distinction; for all have sinned and fall short of the glory of God . . . (Romans 3:21–23).

For the word of the cross is to those who are perishing foolishness, but to us who are being saved it is the power of God. (1 Corinthians 1:18).

Cherished as a symbol for generations, the Cross is a window through which we survey the panorama of God's immeasurable love.

Humankind will never understand the Cross of Christ until they see God at work in it. The meaning of the Cross cannot be perceived by the natural mind until illuminated by the Holy Spirit. When we contemplate the message of the Cross, we embrace it or hate it. Thus, the Cross of Jesus Christ has divided mankind since Calvary.

The good news of the Cross assaults our proud natures. We cannot be justified before God by our own suppositions, works, or excellence. As we stand before the Cross, the commonality of our failure, our sin, is revealed.

Yet, to this preposterous chronicle, Christians cling. It is our glory and exultation.

6

THROUGH THE USE OF A DIGITAL CAMERA, a computer, and appropriate software, parts of photographs were manipulated, pieced, and rebuilt to construct the crosses in this book. The crosses were not made from photographs of jewels or polished metals. Rather, they were shaped from images of everyday objects with diverse textures, forms, and complexities. The artist's intent is to reflect the glory of the crucifixion with manipulated images of industrial machines, worn surfaces, discarded materials, old jackets, and other familiar, tangible forms.

A listless glance at the Cross does not offer a pretty image. It looks unsightly to the casual eye. However, a closer look at the crucifixion of Jesus displays a glorious revelation – the love and saving power of our God who fulfilled a plan of redeeming the world by sacrificing Himself in our place. We are innocent because He assumed our guilt. This odious Cross has become the celebration of the Christian church.

MATCH
MADE

And Jesus answered them, saying, "The hour has come for the Son of Man to be glorified" (John 12:23).

These things Jesus spoke: and lifting His eyes to heaven, He said, "Father, the hour has come; glorify Thy Son, that the Son may glorify Thee" (John 17:1).

Death by crucifixion was invented by barbarians and subsequently used by the Romans. In fact, crucifixion was so excruciatingly cruel and terrible that Roman citizens themselves were exempt from its appalling brutality.

Still, the Cross became the central and cherished symbol of the Christian church. Jesus called the time of His death the beginning of His glorification. His followers see the event as commemorative and glorious. Therefore, we refer to the day of His crucifixion as *Good* Friday.

. . . sin which so easily entangles us . . . (Hebrews 12:1b).

. . . and to wait for His Son from heaven, whom He raised from the dead, that is Jesus, who delivers us from the wrath to come (1 Thessalonians 1:10).

Much more then, having now been justified by His blood, we shall be saved from the wrath of God through Him (Romans 5:9).

THE CHRONICLE OF THE CROSS condemns before it saves. God's wrath against sin is an essential component of His saving message. Without an understanding of God's hostility to evil, God's redemptive act is incomprehensible. When we do not acknowledge sin's role, atonement has no relevance.

Sin arouses God's anger. We often try to ignore this essential fact. Transgressions against God have become merely crimes, sicknesses, and mistakes. Our attitudes of self-reliance, self-development, and self-assurance muffle our awareness of sin's profound seriousness.

A defective knowledge of sin permeates much of the teaching in today's church. Reclaiming sin will prompt us to be more accountable to sin's seduction, making manifest the power and merit of the death and resurrection of Jesus Christ.

A clear view of God and His holiness shatters the ego, humbling the sinner. When believers are convicted of sin, they seek the Savior. As people are set free, the glory of the Cross of Christ shines forth.

I have been crucified with Christ; and it is no longer I who live, but Christ lives in me; and the life which I now live in the flesh I live by faith in the Son of God, who loved me, and delivered Himself up for me (Galatians 2:20).

For the love of Christ controls us, having concluded this, that one died for all, therefore all died (2 Corinthians 5:14).

SIN—WHICH IS WORSHIP OF SELF—is indisputably an important chapter in the chronicle of the Cross. Humankind fancies self-fulfillment, self-reliance, and mastering its own fate. Like Eve in the garden, we do not believe God. We are sinners. Evil resides in our human natures.

Our theme at this juncture of the cross narrative should not read, "I'm okay. You're okay." Rather, it should affirm that "I'm not okay and you're not okay." Nevertheless, God proclaims us "okay" through the "gift by His grace through the redemption which is in Christ Jesus" (Romans 3:24). We are no longer under the shame of the law. We are living by virtue of the grace of our Almighty Father for Christ's sake.

Christians are both fully saint and fully sinner. They face the condemnatory law and live under the affirming gospel of their Almighty God. Believers find themselves periodically perplexed whether good or evil dominates their lives. The comfort of the Cross reassures. The sacrifice of the Cross beckons.

Because our humanity harbors the old nature, God admonishes us to take up our cross and to die to ourselves. Cultivated by sinful nature, our temptations and allurements need to be resolutely rejected. The Christian's cross, not a malady, affliction, or adversity, instead spurns the self-centeredness of our human nature.

Surely our griefs He Himself bore, and our sorrows He carried; yet we ourselves esteemed Him stricken, smitten of God, and afflicted (Isaiah 53:4).

For God so loved the world, that He gave His only begotten Son, that whoever believes in Him should not perish, but have eternal life (John 3:16).

He who did not spare His own Son, but delivered Him up for us all, how will He not also with Him freely give us all things? (Romans 8:32).

For God, forgiveness is a far-reaching, penetrating act. Our righteous God cannot simply dismiss sin. Sin is entirely incompatible with God's holiness and justice. He must express His wrath and expel sin completely – and He did so on the Cross of Christ.

Amazingly, God loves us, the objects of His wrath. Accordingly, God, through Christ, has paid the penalty for our sins. On the Cross, He expressed both justice and mercy by transferring our sins to the Lord Jesus Christ.

Almost incomprehensible is that God redirected His wrath to His only Son.

Some have said that the Jews crucified Christ. Yet, other Christians have said, "No, we all put Jesus on the Cross. I helped place Him there." Both groups are wrong. We do not have the capability to send Jesus to the Cross. We cannot receive any credit for this wondrous act. His Father sent Him there for us, His commitment through all eternity.

I will rejoice greatly in the Lord, my soul will exult in my God; for He has clothed me with garments of salvation, He has wrapped me with a robe of righteousness . . . (Isaiah 61:10).

. . . the temple of God is holy, and that is what you are (1 Corinthians 3:17b).

INDEED, OUR SIN HAS BEEN IMPUTED to Jesus Christ; however, this imputation is not the entire account. A two-fold transfer tells us much more has happened.

Not only did Christ accomplish atonement for our sins, He has also handed over His righteousness to us. We are both cleansed of our sin and clothed in His righteousness. God sees us as sinless and holy. He embraces us as His adopted sons and daughters.

Do you not believe that I am in the Father, and the Father is in Me? The words that I say to you I do not speak on My own initiative, but the Father abiding in Me does His works (John 14:10).

UNITY EXISTS in the story of the Cross.

The idea of a loving Christ who pleads and persuades a reluctant Father to forgive sinners is a false notion. God did not change His mind and heart because of Christ's death on the Cross. It was God's great love that sent Jesus to the Cross in the first place. The Father and Jesus are one. They are in the plan of salvation together.

With the crosses in this book, the repetition of forms, textures, and colors conveys unity and removes discord. Each beam of a cross is equal in design to the other three, contributing to form a unified whole. The compositions' satisfying images complete our perception.

Like a lamb that is led to slaughter . . . (Isaiah 53:7b).

. . . just as it is written, "Let him who boasts, boast in the Lord" (1 Corinthians 1:31).

In a way, the message of the Cross is repulsive and nauseating. God punishes sin with a sentence of death. The necessary shedding of blood smote God's only Son on our behalf. This frightful aspect of the Cross is symbolized on the adjacent page by the ominous cicadas on the four extended arms.

Yet, though hideous, the Cross blazes wonder and glory—astounding! The Christian delights in the Cross's salvation power. That vile Cross has become the triumph and splendor of the Christian church.

But God demonstrates His own love toward us, in that while we were yet sinners, Christ died for us (Romans 5:8).

In this is love, not that we loved God, but that He loved us and sent His Son to be the propitiation for our sins (1 John 4:10).

The Lord your God . . . will exult over you with joy, He will be quiet in His love, He will rejoice over you with shouts of joy (Zephaniah 3:17).

God exposes sin because of His infinite love toward humankind. Only when sin is revealed can the fulfillment of the death of God's Son run its course. The Cross of Christ shows us the essence of God's infinite love – a love that saves us from His wrath at the cost of His only Son.

God is love; therefore, He loves us because of who He is, not because of who we are. From our view, our being contains no commanding merit nor attraction. His love chooses the unworthy. He simply assures us: "I am who I am."

The thoughts and deliberations of Christians should center on how much God loves them, not on how much or little they love Him. Thus, we fix "our eyes on Jesus, the author and perfecter of the faith, who for the joy set before Him endured the cross . . ." (Hebrews 12:2).

Indeed, God delights in His people. His sole reason is that He chooses to do so.

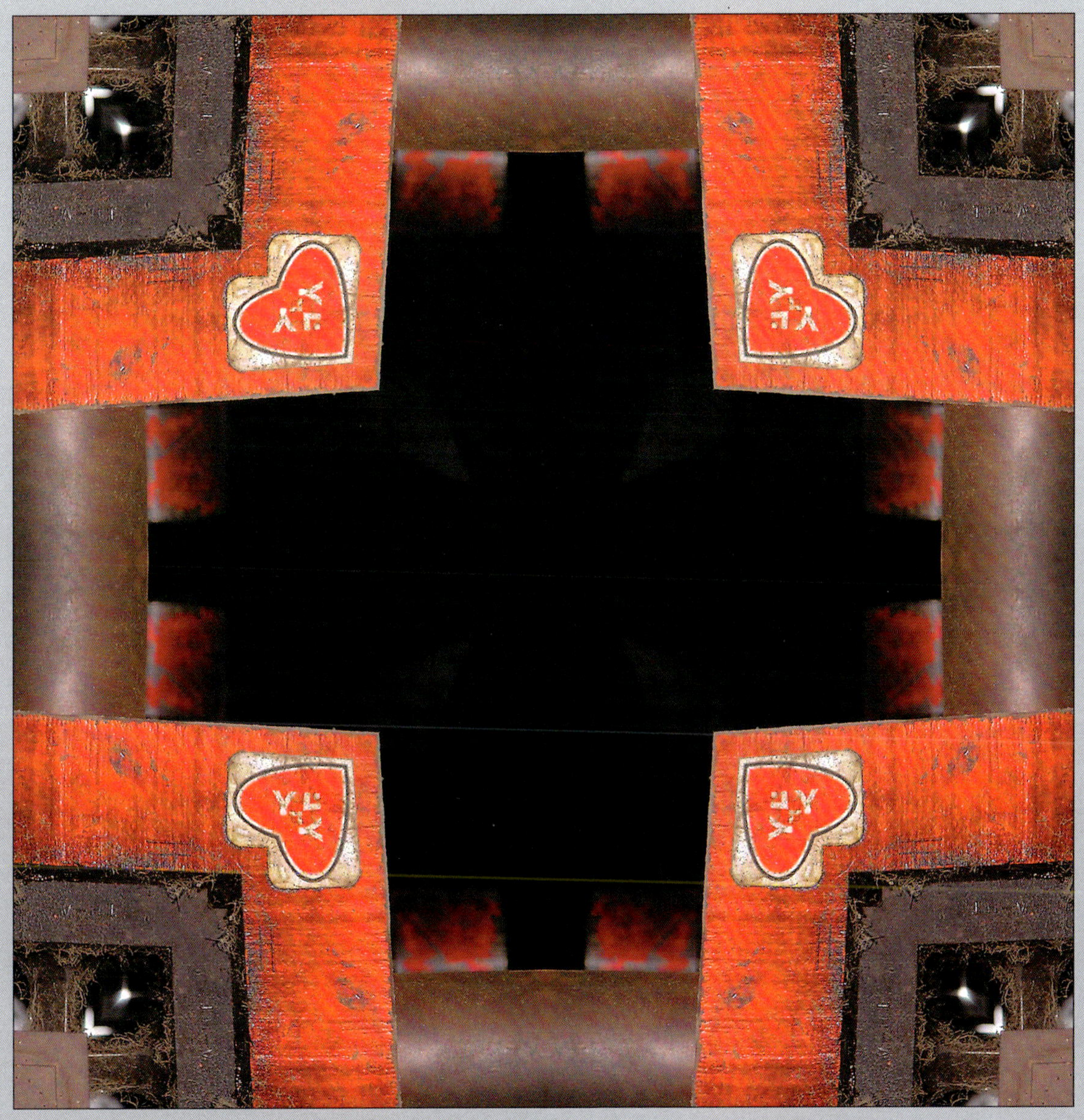

But may it never be that I should boast, except in the cross of our Lord Jesus Christ, through which the world has been crucified to me, and I to the world. (Galatians 6:14).

WE SHOULD BOAST ONLY in the Cross of Christ. Our swagger is not how much we love God, but how much He loves us. This focus is not on a self-centered faith but on our faith in the Savior. The Christian persuasion is belief in the Lord Jesus Christ who bore the Cross for all mankind. Thus, faith finds its worth not in the believer but in the believed One, the crucified Lord and Savior.

Again, the nobility of faith is not in the believer, but in the majesty of the Savior in whom we believe. Our Christian faith directs its attention toward the Lord Jesus Christ, the One who works in us in spite of our erratic expression of faith – the One who redeemed us through an encounter with the Cross. Accordingly, our undivided exultation embraces the Christ.

. . . since the creation of the world His invisible attributes, His eternal power and divine nature, have been clearly seen . . . (Romans 1:20a).

. . . "Sir, we wish to see Jesus" (John 12:21b).

The form of the Cross can be seen everywhere. Justin Martyr, a second-century church father, saw it on the faces of people (the brow being perpendicular to the nose); Malcolm Muggeridge found the Cross in many everyday objects such as two pieces of wood nailed together or a telephone pole.

As we grow in our appreciation of the Cross's significance, we see the world in a new and different way. God's sign of salvation appears around us everywhere. A walk around the block or a trip through a junk yard or the countryside will reveal many visual forms of the Cross. It is simply a matter of seeking them out, as the following portfolio displays.

6 B
6 B

And the Lord said to Abram, after Lot had separated from him, "Now lift up your eyes and look from the place where you are, northward and southward and eastward and westward; for all the land which you see, I will give it to you and to your descendants forever. . . . Arise, walk about the land through its length and breadth; for I will give it to you" (Genesis 13:14, 15, 17).

PAUL EXHORTED TIMOTHY: "Remember Jesus Christ, risen from the dead, descendant of David . . . . " So we must continually gaze upon the Cross of Christ.

But how much time do we spend looking at the Cross – thinking, boasting, and exulting in it? Each of us should carefully examine the Cross. Paul in Ephesians 3:17–19 encourages us to survey and scan it from many viewpoints "so that Christ may dwell in your hearts through faith; and that you, being rooted and grounded in love, may be able to comprehend with all the saints what is the breadth and length and height and depth [inadvertently inscribing the form of a cross], and to know the love of Christ which surpasses knowledge, that you may be filled up to all the fulness of God."

Just as Abram was to gaze with wonder walking the land that God had generously given him, so Christians are to survey and embrace the Cross. The followers of Christ strive to walk through the perplexities of the Cross and note its wonders and surprises. Exploring the diverse textures, forms, and complexities in the following portfolio may well provoke varieties of thought about the miracle of Christ's Cross.

NS
STANDARD-ARC

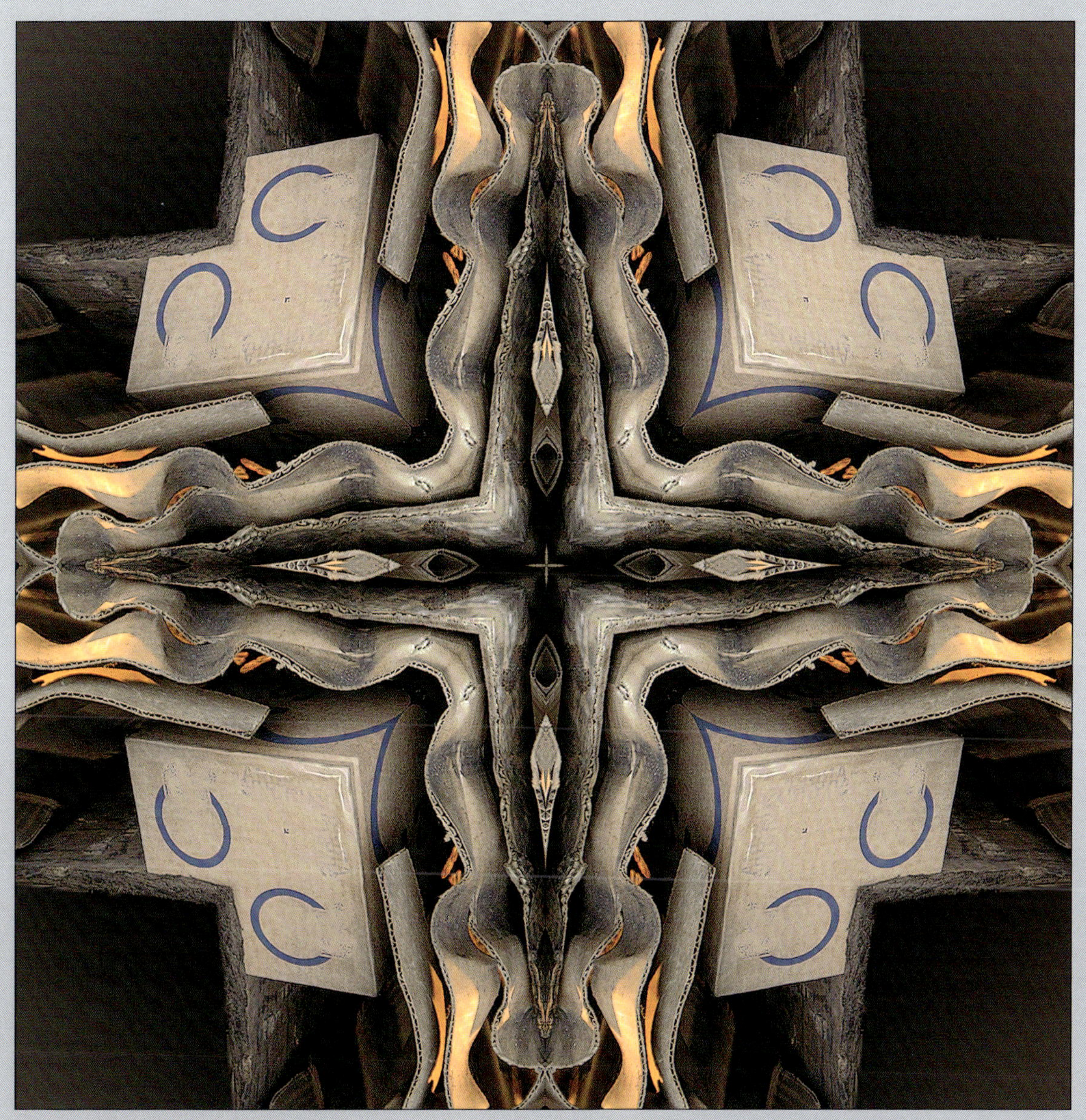

0.000.00

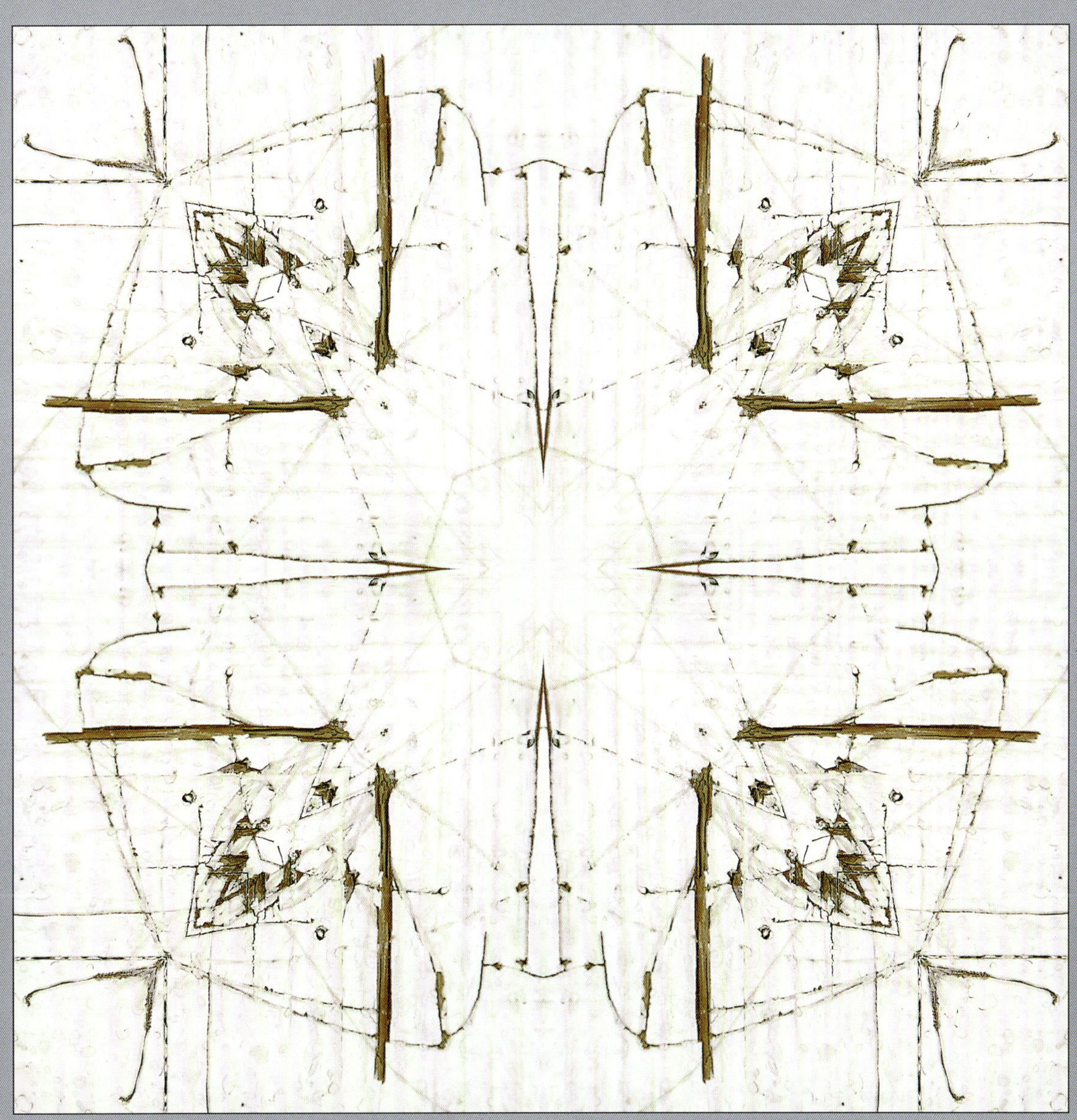

For I determined to know nothing among you except Jesus Christ, and Him crucified (1 Corinthians 2:2).

The Cross of Christ, the core of reality, is vital to history, biblical doctrine, and faithful living. All Christian theology, from creation to the resurrection and beyond, originates from the Cross. Theistic evolution, for example, does not flow from cross theology. It minimizes the significance of the Cross because it does not recognize death as the penalty for sin. Since a key element of evolution is death, we must assume that death occurred before Adam and Eve existed. And, if loss of life happened before our first parents lived and sinned – as an evolutionist must believe – it could not have become the penalty for their transgression. Death was already there. Creation had already been spoiled through the evolutionary process. If this tenet is reliable, that is, if death is not the penalty for sin, the crucifixion is ineffectual. One would have to ask why it was necessary for Jesus to die on the Cross.

The created crosses in this series are of Greek design with arms of equal length. Many people sign their foreheads and hearts with the form of the Greek cross. The sign symbolizes with the hand's downward stroke that Jesus descended from heaven; with the motion of the hand to the left, He died on the Cross; and with the motion to the right, He rose from the tomb.

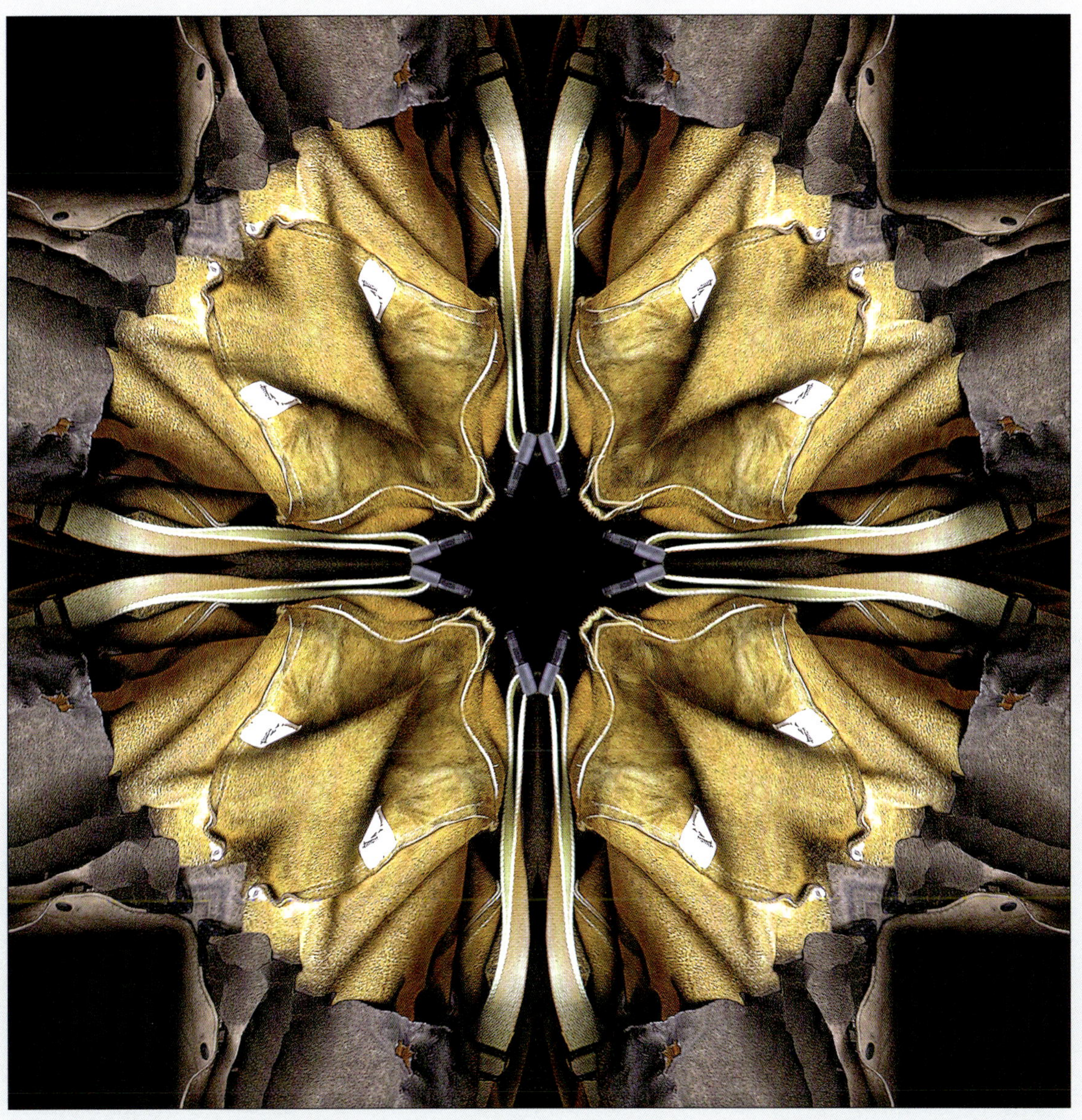

After this I saw four angels standing at the four corners of the earth, holding back the four winds of the earth . . . (Revelation 7:1).

THE CROSSES in this book are placed within a square border. In biblical numerology, the number four symbolizes the world. Like the four-sided square, we speak of the four seasons of the year, the four phases of the moon, and the four directions of the compass. The Bible mentions the four winds and the four corners of the earth.

The number four and the square by themselves, however, represent weakness and inadequacy. Four is the first composite number that can be divided by two and therefore easily broken. Without God's presence, the square is incomplete. Without the invasion of the Cross of Christ, the world is a failure.

> . . . so His appearance was marred more than any man, and His form more than the sons of men (Isaiah 52:14).
>
> But He was pierced through for our transgressions, He was crushed for our iniquities . . . (Isaiah 53:5a).
>
> For this reason the Father loves Me, because I lay down My life that I may take it again. No one has taken it away from Me, but I lay it down on My own initiative. I have authority to lay it down, and I have authority to take it up again. This commandment I received from My Father (John 10:17, 18).

TAUNTING SOLDIERS publicly humiliated Jesus with a mocking crown of thorns, a reed for a scepter, and eventually nakedness on a cross. He was rejected, broken, and executed. His bloody image certainly did not bespeak a king.

The prophet Isaiah has written more about Jesus' agonizing physical condition during the crucifixion than all of the evangelists did. The Gospels simply state that Jesus was crucified. From this scant biblical information, contemporary physiologists have given us a glimpse of that gruesome execution. We are told of the excruciating pain from the scourging that ripped His back, and of the nails driven through the nerves and tendons of His hands, to His lingering death with searing thirst and laborious breathing. Nonetheless, Jesus refused to seek comfort. Rejecting an opiate, Jesus endured pain to its fullest. He could have shortened the time of His suffering but did not.

Even so, physical suffering was not Jesus' cup, but rather He drank to the dregs the spiritual suffering within the very depths of His soul.

Though He slay me, I will hope in Him (Job 13:15).

For I am convinced that neither death, nor life, nor angels, nor principalities, nor things present, nor things to come, nor powers, nor height, nor depth, nor any other created thing, shall be able to separate us from the love of God, which is in Christ Jesus our Lord (Romans 8:38, 39).

But the Lord was pleased to crush Him, putting Him to grief; if He would render Himself as a guilt offering . . . (Isaiah 53:10a).

My God, my God, why hast Thou forsaken me? (Psalm 22:1a).

Terrible as crucifixion was, physical pain was not the full draught of Jesus' cup. It was that of enduring divine judgment – of being forsaken by His Father.

Jesus was more than reverently reciting Psalm 22 at His crucifixion. He was shouting a dire dereliction, imploring His Father in His devastation. Through it all, however, He still addressed His Father in the possessive: "MY God, MY God." Jesus' plea vividly tells us of His awareness of His Father's abandonment. Yet, His plea displays an infinite trust in God amidst the anguished void of response from His Father. His supplication shows His dependence on God even though His Father had handed Him over to be killed.

> . . . the man and his wife hid themselves from the presence of the Lord God among the trees of the garden. Then the Lord God called to the man and said to him, "Where are you?" (Genesis 3:8b, 9).
>
> Christ redeemed us from the curse of the Law, having become a curse for us — for it is written, "Cursed is everyone who hangs on a tree . . ." (Galatians 3:13).

THE NAME, MOST HIGH GOD, underscores God's distance from sin. He cannot tolerate sin and sin cannot stand in His presence. Accordingly, the Father, in justice, retreated from the One who took our sin upon Himself — a rejection imaged by nature's darkness when Jesus died.

Adam's sin compelled him to hide from the Lord. But God in His love pursued Adam and has been pursuing all of His children ever since. To accomplish God's mission, Jesus was made to be sin for us, thus enacting His Father's rejection. In exchange, we have received the righteousness of Christ. Through the activity of the Cross, we are worthy to stand before Him. We do not need to hide anymore.

God, in His love, continues to seek out humankind. In doing so, Christ's death superseded our death; His darkness assumed our darkness. Taking personal responsibility for our wickedness, He was condemned. This shameful, ignominious drama of the Cross reveals how appalling our sin is and how immense God's love is.

Jesus cried out to His Father, but nothing happened. God was silent. Indeed, the Savior died completely. He died accursed of God. Thus, Jesus drank the full draught of suffering unto death.

And this is the message we have heard from Him and announced to you, that God is light, and in Him there is no darkness at all (1 John 1:5).

In Him was life; and the life was the light of men (John 1:4).

The Lord is my light and my salvation; whom shall I fear? (Psalm 27:1a).

For Christ also died for sins once and for all, the just for the unjust, in order that He might bring us to God . . . (1 Peter 3:18).

God is light—the first thing in time that the Creator called into existence was light. God's gift of light is an important theme shining throughout the Bible.

At the time of Jesus' birth, dazzling light dissolved the midnight skies; conversely at noon, during the time of Jesus' death, dreadful darkness pervaded the land. When Jesus died, the light or presence of God withdrew, causing darkness to hold sway. Obscurity prevailed during those formidable three hours. God became inaccessible to His Son.

The light of God's purity exposes sin. He cannot dismiss sin and did not do so at Calvary. The Son of God became sin for us, separating Him from His Father.

Darkness is the absence of light. Darkness can never consume light, but light always overcomes darkness. The Creator has revealed His love to humankind, beaming God's glory from the Cross. God is victorious. We share in this glorious victory.

For to this end Christ died and lived again, that He might be Lord both of the dead and of the living (Romans 14:9).

. . . and if Christ has not been raised, then our preaching is vain, your faith also is vain (1 Corinthians 15:14).

This Jesus God raised up again, to which we are all witnesses (Acts 2:32).

THE FATHER ABANDONED JESUS at the Cross; however, He also raised Him from the dead. The resurrection is an essential chapter in the chronicle of the Cross. If Jesus had not risen, the Christian assurance would have died with Him.

When Jesus predicted His death, He always included the truth that He would rise again on the third day. To the scoffers, this promise seemed foolish; to the disciples, it seemed inexplicable. Indeed, the resurrection was a miracle – an act beyond any natural explanation.

From Calvary's Cross the open tomb now bursts forth. Death has been shattered.

The resurrection confirms and proclaims God's finished work, salvation attained at the Cross. The crosses in this book have no corpora, no dead bodies. A cross displayed without a hanging figure of Christ declares that the redeeming act on the Cross has been completed; it celebrates the resurrection of Jesus from the dead, revealing a finished task that has brought salvation to His people.

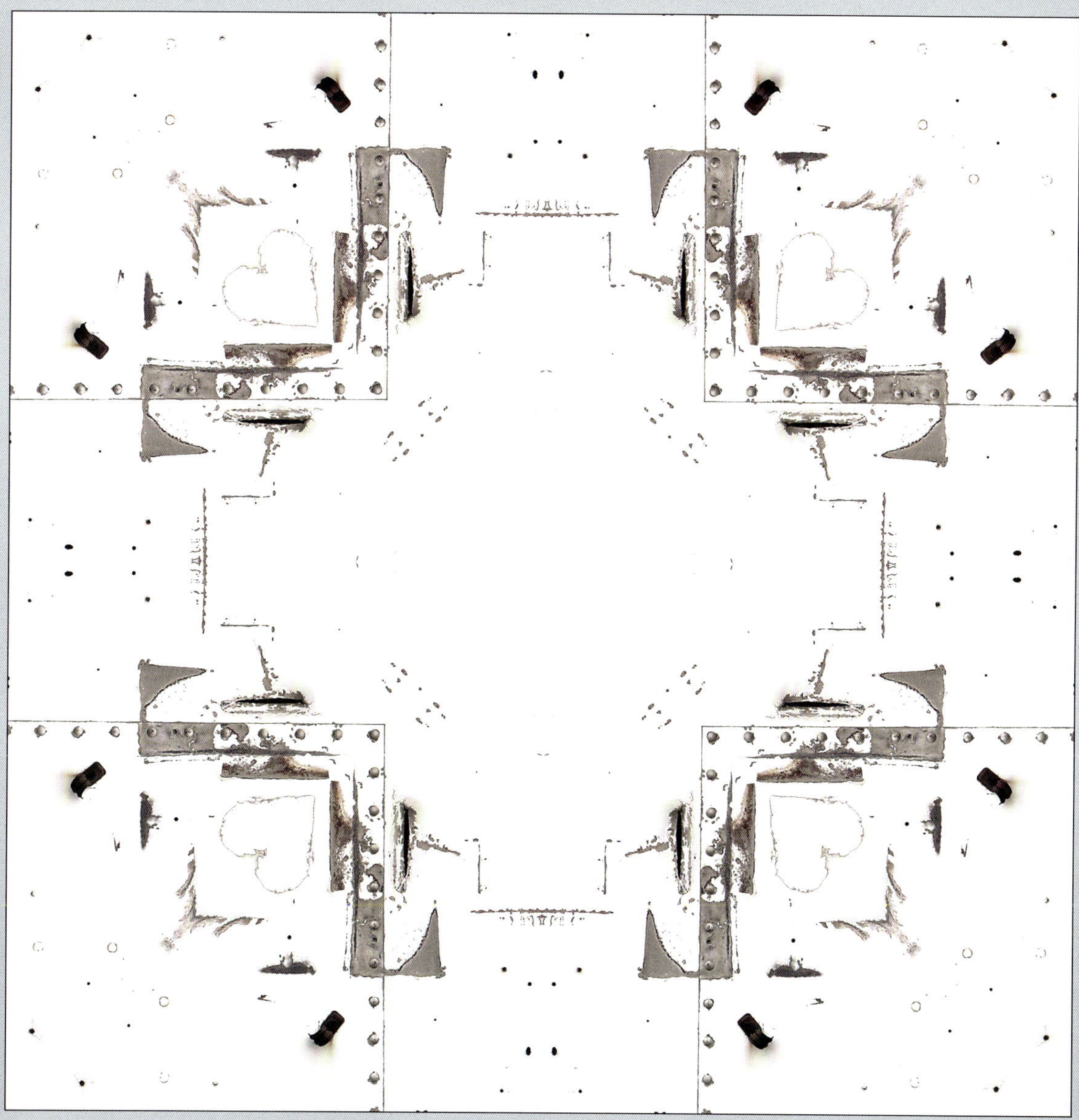

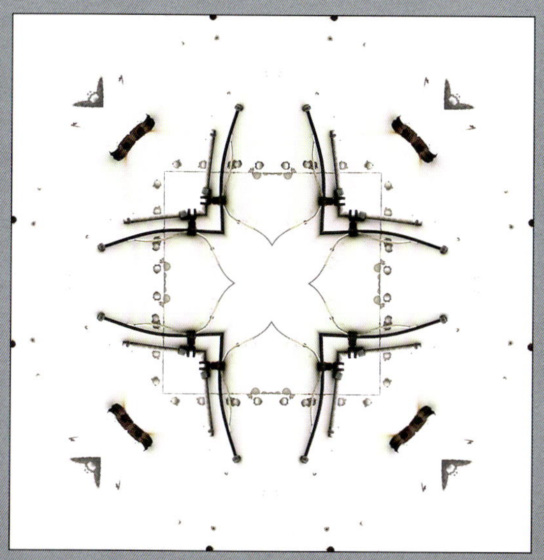
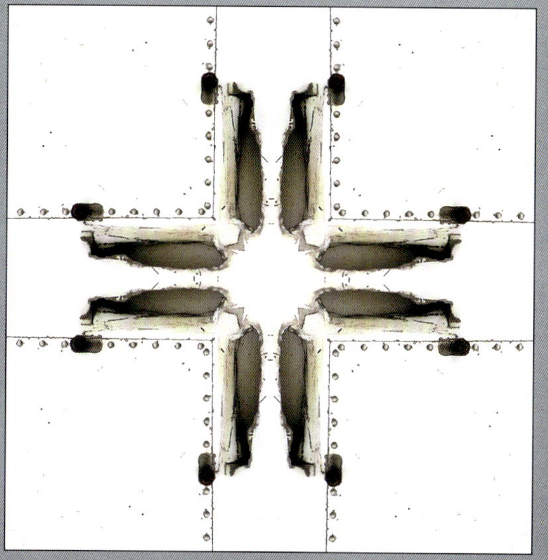

DURING A CRUCIFIXION, a placard that listed the crimes of the executed person was sometimes placed above the cross. Our sins have been placed above the head of Christ and into His whole being, as Paul affirms in Colossians 2:14, ". . . having canceled the written code with its regulations, that was against us and that stood opposed to us; He took it away, nailing it to the cross."

On the cross on the adjacent page, attached notations ascribing our transgressions are worn away. Our sins were nailed to the Cross, but now they have been removed. The list is gone. The work of the Cross is complete.

. . . and He died for all, that they who live should no longer live for themselves, but for Him who died and rose again on their behalf (2 Corinthians 5:15).

Go therefore and make disciples of all the nations, baptizing them in the name of the Father and the Son and the Holy Spirit . . . (Matthew 28:19).

A Greek cross is more three-dimensional than the traditional Latin cross. The Latin rood stands vertically with a limited reach, whereas the Greek cross naturally positions horizontally, reaching in all directions, promoting evangelical activity.

The Greek-style cross on the adjacent page reveals arrows on the arms, representing the attitude of reaching out. Also, it has a forward and backward interchange with the objects in the four corners, further displaying the commission of making disciples of all the nations.

Yet Thou art holy, O Thou who art enthroned upon the praises of Israel (Psalm 22:3).

For Christ our Passover also has been sacrificed. Let us therefore celebrate the feast . . . (1 Corinthians 5:7b, 8).

To be enraged over our sin is a prelude to proper worship. To see oneself as fallen, yet redeemed by God, is paramount for befitting praise. A journey to the Cross and open tomb precedes an ovation to our loving Father. A celebration feast, traditional or contemporary, requires recognizing what God in His love has done for humanity. This necessitates a clear perception of His continuing presence among us knowing we must trust in Him completely.

Is God more present in the chancel of a church than in its narthex? Likewise, is He more present to a believer than to a skeptic? It is only by the power and enlightenment of the Holy Spirit that we cherish the Cross and open tomb and perceive the presence of God in our daily lives.

We cannot evaluate worship by its ability to provoke emotional highs or fascinate inquisitive minds. Worship is neither amusement nor intellectual jugglery about God. It is the continual telling and extolling of that repeatedly forgotten, yet wondrous action—the death and resurrection of the Son of God. It is realizing once again that God has given us the gift of salvation. Therefore, our lives, a continuous, day-by-day celebration, express praise and thanks to our glorious God.

. . . He said, "It is finished!" (John 19:30).

. . . who for the joy set before Him endured the cross, despising the shame, and has sat down at the right hand of the throne of God (Hebrews 12:2b).

. . . He raised Him from the dead, and seated Him at His right hand in the heavenly places . . . (Ephesians 1:20).

The church celebrates together as community and family. The Eucharist is an important component of its celebration. The Lord's Supper, offered at a serving table rather than at an altar, defines a vital part of our worship celebration. Chancel altars imply an unfinished work which denies the sufficiency of Christ's once-for-all sacrifice. We celebrate at a raised slab as we remember His death and resurrection, receiving the forgiveness of our sins and a foretaste of the feast to come. The altar of the Cross has been replaced. Jesus is no longer at Calvary. He is now at His throne. Christ's sacrifice is complete; it is a finished work. He reigns!

And the one who spoke with me had a gold measuring rod to measure the city, and its gates and its wall. And the city is laid out as a square, and its length is as great as the width; and he measured the city with the rod, fifteen hundred miles [twelve thousand furlongs]; its length and width and height are equal (Revelation 21:15, 16).

For to this end Christ died and lived again, that He might be Lord both of the dead and of the living (Romans 14:9).

. . . and He will reign forever and ever (Revelation 11:15e).

THE SQUARE SYMBOLIZES EARTH, where Christ came to dwell. By the power of His death, resurrection, and lordship, the square expands in space and fashions a most perfect form, a cube, symbolizing God's dwelling place. The Holy of Holies in the tabernacle measured ten cubits in each direction; the Most Holy Place in the temple twenty cubits with each dimension; and the New Jerusalem, a place of absolute perfection, twelve thousand furlongs each way. A measure of twelve thousand suggests the Lord Christ's perfect rule – twelve symbolizing His sovereignty and a thousand or ten to the third power, a cubed number, representing a degree of completion, perfection, and rule beyond our comprehension.

God's ultimate and final work of the Cross brings us to His holy city where the mission of Jesus' death, resurrection, and reign are completely realized.